The Happy Cottage: A Tale Of Summer's Sunshine

Annie French Hector

THE HAPPY COTTAGE

A TALE

OF

SUMMER'S SUNSHINE

BY THE AUTHOR OF

"KATE VERNON" "AGNES WARING" &c:

THE ARRIVAL.

LONDON,
T. CAUTLEY NEWBY,
30, WELBECK ST. CAVENDISH SQ.
1856.

TO DEAR PERCY AND EMILY,

WHO FORMED MY FIRST AUDIENCE, THE

FOLLOWING TALE

IS AFFECTIONATELY DEDICATED BY

THE AUTHOR.

THE HAPPY COTTAGE;

OR,

THE POWER OF LOVE.

~~~~~~~~~~~~~~~~

CHAPTER I.

THERE is no pleasanter place in the world to spend the Midsummer holidays in than Fairley Cottage. It is a low, irregular, wide spreading cottage, with projecting eaves, and bow windows peeping out of the eglantine and honeysuckles that climb its wall, and a deep porch, furnished with seats, where you may rest your ship to trim its sails before going to the beach, or arrange your fishing tackle before starting for the river. Softly rounded hills, covered with thick woods, out of which here and there great grey cliffs stand up gauntly, rise behind and about it, and in front the pretty flower garden, so gay with geraniums and salvias, and exquisite moss roses, and sweet with heliotrope and mignonette, is divided by a light paling from the little lawn which stretches beyond. In the centre of this lawn stood a great oak tree, so large that the house and garden might, with a little management, have been packed beneath its spreading branches; but the master of Fairley Cottage was content to place a nice low bench all round the mossy trunk: beyond this still there was a fringe of evergreens and larch trees, through which you caught the sparkle and even heard the gentle dash of the wide blue sea —indeed an opening in the trees, just opposite the drawing-room windows, permitted a view of the waters, with a blue craggy Island in the distance.

If you passed by the vases of flowers, formed of rough wood and filled with mould, which stood before the windows, and kept to the right, you would find another garden at that end of the Cottage, with such quantities of fruit trees, laden with their sweet burdens already ripening in the sun, and luxuriant vegetables; and past this still a door admitted you to a neat yard where cocks and hens crowed and cackled, a dear rough honest donkey sometimes brayed, and a nice respectably kept pig frequently squeaked. There was a dairy, too, though not a large one, for Fairley Cottage boasted but one cow—nevertheless curds and cream were ever plenty, and the sweet fresh butter never failed.

The inside was very pleasant too. There was a smart drawing-room, with gay chintz curtains and worked footstools, pictures and handsomely bound books; but that room was not often used. There was also a parlour, with red curtains and oak pannels, and a dark polished floor on which any one might slip were it not for pathways of red cloth which led from the square of dull Turkey carpet to the door, the sideboard, and the window. Nevertheless it was a pleasant room also, with its stands of flowers and cheerful array of books and work. Beyond these rooms were two smaller ones—the first, a solemn chamber, lined with huge books, littered with papers, and stained with ink, was grandfather's study, it looked upon the vegetable garden; the last, of similar size, with common chairs, a drugget, a cosy grate, a green baize cloth on the table covered with drops of sealing wax and blots of ink; it had hanging book shelves, deal desks, high chairs, and was unmistakeably the school room.

The owner of this pretty cottage was Mr. Crawford, a very old gentleman, as he was considered by his young friends, but still able to walk, and read, and

talk, and ride as far and as fast as
anyone. His daughter, Aunt Mary, as
she was usually called, kept his house,
and seemed to the children as old as her
father; she was a small, neat, cheerful
person, always dressed in black, with a
white cap, so neatly quilted about her
face, that it seemed fairy fingers must
have held the lace; she wore high-
heeled stuff shoes, that you could hear
her going pat, pat all over the house—
for she was a very busy person, whisk-
ing about from parlour to kitchen, from
kitchen to dairy, from dairy to store-
room, and the children thought her time
well spent when they ate the nice hot
cakes, the tarts, puddings, custards, and
endless good things that came out of
that store-room of hers. Moreover, a

great work-basket always stood by her low arm chair in the parlor, where quantities of coarse cotton and woollen materials were always ready to be made up, while everything that the heart of boy or girl could desire was to be found there, from bits of twine and bees' wax, and reels of every coloured cotton, to the most desirable scraps of waste paper, and a perfect treasury of rags, only no one must touch it without her leave.

These children were Fred and Dora, the orphans of Mr. Crawford's only son, and they are now just finishing their afternoon lessons with their governess, Miss Chapman, a very kind grave lady, whom they loved very much, though they never teased her as, I fear, they sometimes did Aunt Mary.

Fred was a thoughtful, pale, delicate boy of seven years old, by no means pretty, and his sister a year older. Though she had the sweetest, softest blue eyes you ever saw, and quantities of glossy curly brown hair, she was deformed; that is, instead of being able to stand straight up, had a rounded back, that bent her pretty head forward, and never would let her have the graceful appearance that is so pleasant to the eye. Nothing could cure this, she was born so, and all her kind friends could do was to instruct her in that " beauty of holiness," that loving obedience to the will of God, which can make the heart and life so lovely, that the mere faultiness of face and form are forgotten.

But with all the kind care of those around her, Dora was often grieved to hear rude boys call her 'little hump-back' as she passed, and although she knew she could not help it, and that those she loved, loved her as much as if she was beautiful, she often cried bitterly when she was alone, and was only comforted by remembering that though her form was crooked her heart was straight, so long as she loved God and "her neighbour as herself."

The morning, about which we begin our story had been very warm, the sun shone so brightly that even puss sought the shade; the garden was all alive with the hum of insects, and great bees were constantly flying into the room, and knocking themselves, with a loud buzz, against the upper pane of the open window. Dora had been reading, and Fred having finished his sums was drawing a picture on his slate.

"That will do, my dear," said Miss Chapman to Dora, "you need not read any more; get your bonnet, we will go down to the beach, the sun must be off it by this time."

"Yes, Miss Chapman, but tell me what did grandpapa mean at dinner to-day?"

"What do you mean?" asked her governess, smiling.

"You know he was talking to you and Aunt Mary, something about the trouble of having such a boy in the house, but he felt he must invite him and you did not seem to like him, nor Aunt Mary."

" Oh, you mean Harry Vigors—poor boy, he has been very unfortunate."

" Was he—how?" asked Fred, leaving his drawing, to listen.

" He was sent home from India to a very proud and rich old lady, his grand-mama, who let him do anything he liked, unless she happened to be cross, and then she punished him severely; she died, and he was sent to school, where they flogged him, but he got worse, and now his uncle does not know what to do, so your grandpapa intends to ask him here."

" Why?" asked Fred, uneasily.

" Because he thinks I can do him some good; and Harry's papa was the dearest friend your papa had, but I confess I was selfish enough not to wish so very naughty a boy to come here."

"I am sure I hope he may not," said little Fred.

"But, Miss Chapman, does he not love some one?" asked his sister.

"Why, my dear?"

"I mean, is there no one he loves enough to try and please, and be good for?"

"I am sure I cannot tell," said Miss Chapman; "perhaps no one loves him —but come, get on your things, there is a sweet fresh breeze coming in with the tide; perhaps Aunt Mary will bring down her work—go and ask her, Fred, while Dora puts away the books."

They were soon ready and passing through the yard, which was always

cool and pleasant, because a great wal-
nut tree stood in the middle, and under
it, a sort of spring or fountain poured
from a stone cistern into a pond where
the ducks were always paddling about;
they called Wowsky, a pet little terrier,
who was too warm to gnaw the bones
lying by his kennel, to follow them,
crossed the vegetable garden, where
John the gardener, who also took care
of the donkey, was spreading nets over
the cherries, and entered a shady shrubbery which led to a gate in the wooden
paling outside the grounds, and then
followed a path that led to the top of
the rocks over the sea; some rough
steps led to the beach, and here the
children began to gather and select the
prettiest pebbles, and all the rarest sea-

weed they could find, for Miss Chapman used to make such pretty patterns of them, with gum, on cardboard—Dora had numbers of them in her box of treasures. There was a hollow, too, under a great, black, smooth rock, which they called their cave, and liked to dress out with all kinds of shells. Dora read there sometimes, and Fred too, often learned his lessons there in the summer time.

Dora, however, soon tired of gathering the seaweed, and Fred saw her standing by the water watching the little rippling waves, clear and bright, that stole in one after the other and swept out again with a gentle murmuring lazy sound. "What are you looking at, Dora?" he asked at last.

"Oh! that beautiful jelly fish!" he added, looking at a splendid lilac sea anemone that was opening its star-like form under the water.

"No; I did not see it. I was thinking."

"What of?"

"That boy Miss Chapman says is coming here. Fred, what a strange boy he must be to be always naughty."

Fred nodded.

"Perhaps if we were very, very kind, and sorry for him, he might be better, I am half afraid of him."

"I am, too. I wish he might not come," cried Fred. "Perhaps he may break my new boat that Captain Morton gave me, or hurt poor Wowsky."

"Yes, Fred; but then his Papa was a great friend of ours, and perhaps if he comes he may learn to be a good boy from Miss Chapman."

"Perhaps," said Fred doubtingly.

But the sound of voices shouting "Dora,"—"Fred,"—made them look round, and they saw with great pleasure Charlie and Frank Morton, with their sister Catherine, running to meet them. These little friends were the children of Captain and Mrs. Morton, who lived in a splendid Castle on a hill, about a mile from Fairley Cottage. They were very fond of Dora and Fred, and the children often played together on the beach. They agreed very well, and although Captain Morton was very rich —far richer than Mr. Crawford—and his children had ponies to ride and carriages to drive in, I do not think

Fred or Dora ever fancied it would be the least bit better to live at the Castle instead of the Cottage.

But the arrival of their friends put Harry out of their heads, and they thought no more about him.

At last they were called in to tea, and very much they enjoyed that meal after a day of wholesome work and play. Grandpapa, a stout grave, gay old gentleman, with keen dark eyes like his daughter's, and an air of great authority, was peculiarly silent. At length, as they were rising from table, he said, " Stay a moment children; come to me. You know I expect a little boy on a visit here."

" Yes, grandpapa."

" I am informed by a letter I received

to-day that we may look for him to-morrow. I am sorry you have heard a bad account of him, for it may make you proud and disdainful towards him when he arrives, but I hope you will forget all, and just behave to him as if he was the best boy in the world—remember he has not shewn himself naughty to us yet. Besides, if you look into your own hearts and think of the bad tempers that attack you sometimes, and how little you could do to conquer them if you had no guide to lead you to pray for God's help, no steady friend, like Miss Chapman, to strengthen your habits of self-denial—you will see you have no right to look down on this poor boy, who was first brought up in India among ignorant, though kind, black

servants, who let him do what he liked,
and then sent to a proud old lady whom
illness had made severe. But let us
endeavour to show him the happiness and sweetness of obedience from
Love."

"I should like to," said Fred, "if he
will not break my ship or tear my
pictures."

"I hope he will not," replied grandpapa.

Dora said nothing. She did not like
to speak of what she feared. She only
kissed grandpapa's hand as it hung over
the arm of his chair, and looked up so
lovingly with her soft blue eyes, where
the beauty of a gentle heart looked out,
that grandpapa took her on his knee and
kissed her twice, and then he told Fred

to bring his high chair and the large map of Europe, and traced his travels from England to the Tyrol, describing what he had seen, till it was time to go to bed.

CHAPTER II.

You may imagine with what impatience Dora and Fred watched for Harry the next day. It was not certain how soon he would come, as it was a long way from Fairley to the nearest coach or railway, therefore both the children nearly wore themselves out, and Miss Chapman too, with questions and conjectures.

At half-past one, they sat down to dinner as usual, and before they had finished Dora suddenly laid down her knife and fork—"Do you not hear the carriage, Aunt Mary?" she asked.

"Finish your dinner, my dear, and never mind," said Aunt Mary.

"Hark! I hear it," crid Fred.

"And I," said Grandpapa. "It must be Harry!"

So every one forgot their dinner, and turned to look at the window, and presently a yellow chaise drove up to the garden gate. Out of it stepped a large portly gentleman, who began immediately to give directions about taking down a trunk, to John, who had come forward as soon as he heard the carriage; and after him, a boy much taller and seemingly older than Dora, stood an instant on the top step, looked round him, and then jumped down—

put his hands in his pockets, and began to whistle. Little Wowsky the terrier, accustomed to children, ran up to him, but the young gentleman gave him an angry kick, and then shrank to the fat gentleman's side as if half afraid. "Oh, Aunt Mary — Miss Chapman!" cried Fred; "he has hurt Wowsky! How I wish he might not come here!"

"Hush, hush, Freddy," said Aunt Mary; and the next moment the door opened, and the gentleman entered, holding Harry by the hand.

"Very happy to see you and your nephew, Mr. Alford," said grandpapa, going forward to greet the strangers with his own kind cordial manner. "My daughter," he continued, introducing her. "Shake hands, Harry. I hope

D

you will like Fairley Cottage. Here, Miss Chapman, is another little boy for you, who will, I hope, find himself as happy in your school-room as Dora and Fred do. Here is a brother and a sister for you, my dear," concluded the good old gentleman, leading Harry up to the two children, who regarded him shyly, with some awe; he shook hands sulkily as he was directed, and then stood quite still, without removing his cap. Harry, though tall, was very thin and pale, with large black eyes and thick curly black hair. Dora thought him very pretty, though not pleasant looking.

Meantime Mr. Alford was talking very fast in a thick voice to Miss Crawford, of the journey from London, and how hurried he was.

"You must require refreshment after your travels," she said. "Pray sit down; there shall be some hot potatoes brought in a moment; and though I fear we have nothing to offer you but some cold beef, I hope you will be able to dine: had we any idea you would have been so early, we should have waited dinner."

"Do not say a word about it, my dear Madam, I am sure you and Mr. Crawford are very good indeed to take charge of this troublesome boy. It is more than Mrs. Alford would do, I can tell you. Come, Harry, sit down to your dinner, and take off your cap, sir. I am sure neither Master nor Miss Crawford ever saw a young gentleman keep on his hat in a dining-room before!"

"It is not a hat, it's a cap," returned

Harry, contemptuously, and throwing it down.

"Don't talk to me, sir, in that tone: how dare you," cried his uncle, as well as he could, for he had just taken a mouthful of very hot potatoes.

"A glass of wine after your hot drive, Mr. Alford," said grandpapa, to divert his attention—and so dinner went on. Harry eat very little meat, and a great deal of plum pie, with cream; and then Mr. Alford and Mr. Crawford went to the study for a little while; and when they came to the dining-room Mr. Alford had his hat in his hand; he bid Miss Crawford and Miss Chapman good bye, and patted Dora's head, kissed Fred, and then turning to Harry— "Good bye to you, sir," he said. "I have told Mr. Crawford he may do what he likes with you—flog you, or lock you up, as you deserve—only to mind and not let you teach these good children to be as naughty and wicked as yourself."

Harry neither hung his head nor held it up; his pale cheek grew a little red, but he looked indifferent and sullen.

"Oh, we have no floggings here," said Mr. Crawford, cheerfully. "And I am sure Harry will excuse them."

"Well, well! I hope you may make something of him," said Mr. Alford; and again wishing them good bye, he stepped into the chaise, and drove away.

Both Dora and Fred felt it was a little frightful to have this terrible boy left behind, but there was no help for it.

"Come, my dears," said Miss Chapman; "let us show Harry his own room and the school-room, and the garden, and then we will go to the beach; you shall have the rest of the day a holiday."

"I thought these were the midsummer holidays," said Harry.

"So they are," replied Grandpapa; "the children do not learn so much as during the winter, but we have no idleness at Fairley Cottage."

Away they went, therefore, and showed Harry his room—a pretty little chamber, next Miss Chapman's, looking out on the blue sparkling sea, with a little projecting window where the eglantine clustered in white starry masses.

Harry thought it very nice, and sweet.

and cool; the little snowy bed looked so
tempting, that he thought he should
like to lie down and sleep, but he was
so vexed at what his uncle had said of
him before these strangers, that he could
not bear to speak.

"Shall we unpack your trunk, Harry?"
asked Miss Chapman, not knowing exactly what to say next.

"Yes, if you like," he replied, for he
was not a little proud of all his fine
clothes—and toys—and pretty things;
so the children in great glee set to work;
Fred and Harry pulled out the things,
and Dora helped Miss Chapman to lay
them neatly in the drawers, and gra-
dually Fred and Harry began to talk
about the toys, and by the time Harry's
things were settled, they were tolerably

good friends; then Fred, in his turn, took Harry to show him the school-room, which Harry by no means admired. "At grandmamma's," he said, "my school-room had a mahogany table, all carved, and book-cases with glass doors, and cushions on the chairs; this table," lifting up the cloth, "is only deal."

"It holds the desks and books very well," said Fred, simply; "but if another kind is better perhaps grandpapa will get one."

What between the new places and the beach, and the garden, and the interest with which his new friends listened to his accounts of grandmamma's fine house, Harry got on very well, and soon after tea he was so tired that Mr.

Crawford desired he should go to bed
without waiting for prayers; so he bid
them good night, and let Anne, the
nurse, put him quietly to bed. She
thought she heard him crying, as he
said his prayers, but she was not sure,
and did not like to take any notice; he
begged she would not take away the
candle before he went to sleep, and so
she left it there.

Thus ended Harry's first day at
Fairley Cottage.

Every one was ready for breakfast,
and Dora and Fred, with Aunt Mary,
had been round the shrubbery, while
the dew yet lay on the trees and flowers
—but still Harry did not make his appearance. At length, just as Mr. Crawford came from the study to the dining-

room, and the great bible was placed ready for him to read, Harry ran into the hall—his hair very untidy, and still buckling his belt, followed by Anne, who cried to him to stop till she brushed his hair. " Do not mind this morning," said grandpapa; " travellers must be excused for being a little late. How are you, Harry, quite rested I hope?" and the old gentleman shook hands with him, and so did Aunt Mary and Miss Chapman, but Dora thought his eyes looked a little red as if he had been crying, and in the kindness of her heart, she offered him a kiss, but he pushed her rudely back, and looked so contemptuously at her that little Dora's cheek grew red and her throat swelled, with a feeling of regret and humiliation, but no one noticed the incident, for all now knelt down to prayer.

Then there was the cheerful breakfast, at which grandpapa spoke a great deal to Harry, asking him what he learnt at school. Harry said he learned a great deal, and was so accustomed to be taught by gentlemen that he did not think he should like to learn from a woman.

Mr. Crawford smiled good-humouredly at this. "Well, my little man," said he, "I suppose you disdain learning with Dora and Fred; so I promise you, if you know so much more than they do, as not to be able to study with them, that you shall have a tutor all to yourself."

"Thank you, Sir," said Harry, in

a grand way.   "Shall *you* examine me?"

"I believe I may trust that undertaking to Miss Chapman," returned grandpapa.

It was full time to go to the schoolroom, and when there, Dora and Fred began as usual to help Miss Chapman to place the books and slates on the table.   "Go, my dear, and fetch your books and slate," said Miss C. to Harry.   "I left them altogether in your room."

"Why may not the servant go for them?"

"Because here every one does as much as possible for themselves—and because I desire it."

Whether Miss Chapman's quiet gentle tone, so decided, and yet not at all cross, induced him to obey, or that he was in a good humour, I cannot tell; but he brought his books, and after some grumblings, settled himself at the table. As usual, the studies began by writing dictation, whereat Harry was rather inattentive. When this was over Miss Chapman set sums for the other children; and while they were busy, called Harry quietly to her, and pointed out to him that nearly every word in his dictation was wrong. "Yes! but I was not minding," said Harry.

"That is the worst excuse you can give," replied Miss Chapman. "Now that you *are* minding, spell them for me;" and she proceeded to make him spell the words off, but he could do it no better. "Well, Harry, you shall learn all these

words for me by to-morrow, or if that
be too much, eight of them ; now let me
see what you can do in the way of
sums."

Harry set to work, but he looked up
soon to see what Dora was doing, and
made a face at her, which made Fred
laugh. Then Miss Chapman told him
to mind his sum; meantime she looked
at Dora's and Fred's. At last she
called Harry: he had not half done his,
and it was wrong. "Get your poetry
and history books," said Miss Chapman
to the other children, and she proceeded
most patiently to explain to Harry the
way in which he ought to do his sum.
But he would not give his mind to the
lesson, and he could not therefore understand — then he got impatient :

"What makes you give me such difficult sums," he said; "you let them,"
pointing to the children, "do easy ones
that are sure to be right, but it is
different with me."

Miss Chapman just drew over the
slates. Dora's was exactly the same,
and Fred's, though not the very same
figures, seemed equally difficult.

At this sight Harry was so mortified;
he flew into a dreadful rage.   He seized
Miss Chapman's dress and tried to tear
it, and strike her, calling out, "You
nasty ill-natured thing, I hate you: I
don't care for you.   What, are you to
teach me! and I hate this nasty mean
place;" with a great deal more, and
with such a noise of screaming, that
Fred was quite frightened, and began

to cry, while Dora, nearly as much
frightened, ran to help Miss Chapman.
"Keep away, love," said that lady, "he
may hurt you."

"Yes," cried Harry, "you want to
help her, you ugly creature, with a
lump on your back!   I'll kill you."

"Oh, dear! Miss Chapman, is he
mad?" asked poor Fred.

"No," said Miss C., quietly.   "Harry,
you have made noise enough; now tell
me what it is all about.   What do you
want: what are you screaming for?"

And Harry, finding himself neither
shaken nor flogged, nor scolded loudly,
began to wonder what he was screaming for, and suddenly stopped.

"You know," he said, sullenly.

"Indeed I do not; think quietly for

a moment, and then go to your room. Ask God to give you a better temper; and when you are in your right mind come down again."

"Why did you show me those sums? but I do not want to go away."

"Then you must learn not to scream for nothing. I am sorry to send you away, for we are going to read a very charming book."

"Please let him stay, Miss Chapman, this time," whispered Dora, "He does not know yet how good and kind and wise you are—and he is a stranger. Ah, yes, let him stay!" Fred said nothing, but dried his tears.

"Well, Harry," said Miss Chapman, "as Dora asks for you, although you have not spoken kindly or even like a gentleman to her, you may."

Harry looked very sulky: it humiliated him to be interceded for by poor Dora. The reading went on, however, and when it came to his turn, he read very badly, and wanted to be allowed to stop very soon—but Miss Chapman made him go on.

After this he was set with the other children to draw—a pleasant and amusing occupation, suited to holiday employment—during which Miss Chapman told them of painters and paintings, and answered their questions ; but Harry soon got tired, and then Miss Chapman allowed him to stop; as both Dora and Fred, however, wished to go on, he found himself very stupid. At last Miss Chapman told them they might go and play in the front of the house, which, looking towards the west, was cool at this hour, and Harry ran off gaily.

"Will you not ask Miss Chapman's pardon?" said Dora.

"Why need I—she lets me go to play without."

"But I could not be happy if I had vexed her !"

"Do not you preach," said Harry, fiercely.

"Oh, is he not naughty!" cried Fred.

"If we could but get him to love us !" said Dora, mournfully, "he would grow good ; now he seems to care only for himself."

In front of the house, between two

fine elm trees, was a swing where
Fred liked to—very much: and Dora a
little.   It was very nicely arranged,
with a chair to sit in, and a rope to pull
by; as soon as Harry saw this; he cried
" There's a swing—that is jolly !" and
away he ran; he soon called Fred and
Dora to swing him; they complied:
but Fred got tired presently, and
walked away to a favorite resort of his,
where he was building what he called
a house, with loose stones and sticks,
behind some laurel trees that hid all
this untidyness.

" Come back, sir," shouted Harry;
" do you hear? come back and swing
me !"

" I am tired; and I do not choose !"
replied Fred.

Harry was out of the swing in a moment, and ran at Fred lifting up his arm to strike him; Fred stopped, and, unaccustomed to such rudeness, burst out crying; but before he could strike, Harry's arm was caught by Dora: "Oh, Harry, do not hurt Fred—he is so gentle, and so much smaller than you are. I will swing you; but do not, do not be so unkind as to hurt Fred—he never meant to vex you."

"Why did he speak so rudely? I would not mind swinging him if he asked nicely," sobbed Fred.

Harry had been for a moment startled by Dora's gentle words and soft, entreating eyes, but the next, he turned from his good thoughts, and said—

"Well, you stupid, ugly little thing,

you shall swing me twice as long, if I do not beat Fred. What cowards you are—you are afraid even to tell of me."

"No, Harry," said Dora, her eyes filling with tears, "I do not wish you to be punished—I want you to be happy like Fred and me."

But though Harry could not help thinking that this was wonderful, and not at all like what he would have done, he hardened his heart, like wicked Pharaoh, and went back to the swing. Dora pulled it backwards and forwards till she was quite tired—"I tell you, you do not do it right," he cried at length springing to the ground; "do you get in, I will show you how."

As soon as Dora was in the swing, he began to pull the rope so violently,

that Dora was flung up ever so high,
till she screamed with terror: but
Harry only laughed, calling her a coward; however, poor Dora soon got so
giddy, that she could not hold on, and
so fell out on the grass ; fortunately, the
swing was near the ground, or she might
have been killed: as it was, she lay a
moment quite still, and Harry looked
at her more than half frightened. Dora
then slowly rose, and feeling very angry
with Harry, was inclined to run to Miss
Chapman and tell of his naughtiness;
but she thought, "it will only make
him hate me, and then he will grow
worse and worse;" and she remembered
how our blessed Saviour desired us to
forgive not only seven times, but
seventy times seven.

"You may go tell," said Harry, uneasily.

"Oh! no, no; you did not mean to hurt me—surely you did not mean it: and if so, it was but an accident," said Dora, crying.

"No; I did not mean to," said Harry, feeling very strange—not fierce and bitter, but sulky and ashamed. "Are you hurt?"

"Not much: the grass is soft. Will you come away from the swing, and see Fred build his house; you can find stones enough for yourself—you shall be the mason, and I will be your man."

This pleased Harry; and they amused themselves very well till dinner time.

Harry was very uncomfortable at dinner; he expected every moment that Dora would tell, but not an unpleasant word was said. Harry made a hearty dinner; and when they were rising from table, Aunt Mary informed them, they were all invited to spend the afternoon at the Castle; and that Frank was to drive over with his mama about four o'clock, to fetch them.

"Come into the school-room, my dears," said Miss Chapman, "and read or draw—but keep quiet till Mrs. Morton calls."

So the three children kept tolerably quiet with her; for Harry was very curious to know what and who the Mortons were; and Fred was eager to describe all the beautiful things at Morton Castle; and then Harry, not to

be outdone, told Fred what a fine
house his grandmama's was, and how
he had everything he liked, etc., etc.

Mrs. Morton arrived a little after
four, in such a pretty pony phaeton,
drawn by two such tiny white ponies,
that you might think they had drawn
Cinderella's fairy coach.

Mrs. Morton was a tall, handsome
lady, with fair hair, and a very sweet
smile. She went into the drawing room
with Miss Crawford; and the three
children put on their hats and gloves,
to be ready; while Frank was full of a
great ship his papa had brought him
from London, which they were to sail
on the Lake that evening.

At length, Mrs. Morton came out of
the drawing room, and called her young

THE DRIVE WITH M^{RS} MORTON.

friends; she took very little notice of the boys, but kissed Dora, and stroked her bright curls. "Come along, children," said she, and made Dora and Fred sit beside her.

"You two young gentlemen in the rumble," cried she, laughing, "hold-on, and sit steady, for if you fall off, I will not stop to pick you up;" so saying, she took the reins and whip, and drove off.

It was a heavenly summer's evening; the sun still glowing brightly, and the shadows just beginning to lengthen. The sweet—sweet new-mown hay, smelling so deliciously behind the hedges—the mossy banks covered with a wealth of wild blossoms—and here and there, the pleasant, measured ringing sound of sharpening the scythe, came to them on the soft breeze. Dora felt unspeakably happy: for her heart was at rest, and felt in tune with the lovely scene—for it was full of love, and therefore at peace.

CHAPTER III.

MORTON CASTLE was a tall, stately building, covered with ivy, and surrounded by a double bank, sloping up right and left from a gravel walk, where once the waters of a wide moat had spread in those unhappy times, long ago, when people were obliged to fortify their dwellings against their own countrymen, as if they were enemies.

The two little Mortons who were playing in front of the castle as our friends drove up, greeted them very warmly. Immediate preparations were made to launch the new ship, which was indeed, very handsome—rigged like a frigate; with guns, and even tiny sailors on the deck and in the shrouds. A tall footman carried it down to a beautiful lake at the end of the gardens on the other side of the castle—and Mrs. Morton telling them to be good children, went in to dinner.

Harry was half surprised to see how kind and gentle Charlie Morton was to Fred and Dora; and Harry, himself, was uncommonly good: in the first place, he was thoroughly amused and excited, and next, everything was so grand and yet so kindly at the castle, that he could neither feel proud nor mortified. The ship sailed very well; and for

more than an hour the children watched
it from side to side, when, suddenly,
just as Miss Johnson, the Mortons'
governess, was telling them it was time
to go into tea, a great curly, black and
white dog came rushing to the place
where they stood, barking with all his
might, he nearly knocked down Fred,
who only laughed, and made for Harry,
who could not help crying with fright,
while he raised a stick he held to strike
the animal; but, to his astonishment,
poor little Dora, whom he despised as
a coward, threw herself before him, and
almost on the fierce dog, calling out—
"Do not strike him, Harry—he will
hurt you if you do!"—and then the
footman called off the dog. Harry
stood quite ashamed; and Charlie

Morton cried—" Dora, you're a brave girl; why, Harry Vigors was frightened !"

" But," said Dora, smiling gently, " I know poor Carlo never intends to hurt any one; and Harry never saw him before—it is quite different !"

" Of course it is !" said Harry, never seeing or caring for Dora's kind defence of him, and thinking only of self. " Even Fred was not afraid !"

" I can tell you, Fred is a brave little boy, though he does look pale and delicate," said Miss Johnson, taking his hand kindly: Fred replied by one of his quiet, happy smiles—contented to be loved; and not-at-all anxious to be clever or thought much about.

Harry, rather vexed at what had

occurred, walked sullenly towards the house with the rest; he wanted little Catherine, a pretty, bright, fair-haired child, to hold his hand, but nothing would induce her to leave Dora, who whispered—"Do, dear Catherine, give him your hand—you know he is a lonely stranger."

But Harry overheard this, and was more vexed than ever. It mortified his foolish pride to be pitied by a little deformed girl, whom he despised; and he said to himself—"She thinks she may treat me as a poor, forlorn creature, but I will show her how little I care for her. I will vex her yet!"

Now, as you read this story quietly, without anything to raise your tempers, I dare say, you say in your hearts, what a naughty, bad boy Harry was, but suppose you had been always whipped and threatened whenever you did what was wrong, or troublesome, and, at the same time, were allowed to speak rudely to servants, and break things when you were cross, and thought people liked to punish you and did not care for your grief, do you think your heart, too, would not be hardened?

I think it would; and, like Harry, you would be inclined to imagine every one an enemy, who was ready in some way to mortify you; or a submissive servant whom you might treat with contempt, while all you cared for would be "*self.*"

Tea, however, went over very tranquilly; there was so much cake, that

Harry eat more than was good for him, without interfering with anyone else's wishes; and after tea, they went out of doors again, to play in the garden. When they were tired of hide-and-seek, etc., Charlie suddenly taking up a stick that lay near, exclaimed—" I am papa looking at the gardeners!" and he began to imitate Captain Morton so well, that even Miss Johnson laughed—and then little Catherine said she was Miss Crawford, and so on ; but Harry, who had run off for a few moments, now returned—he had rushed to the house, seized a small shawl that lay on the sofa, and thrust it under his coat, between his shoulders, where it made a sort of hump—" Now," said he, bending down his head, and trying

to look very demure; " now I am
Dora."

There was a sudden pause—no one
laughed—and then Dora, hiding her
face in her hands, shrank behind Miss
Johnson, and cried quietly, but, oh! so
bitterly. When Charlie Morton saw
this, his eyes flashed with fire—" You
rude, ill-natured boy," he cried, and
flying at Harry, gave him a great blow,
which Harry immediately returned:
and while Miss Johnson was trying to
separate them, Captain Morton came
up. He was a tall, stately gentleman,
with a thick moustache, and a stern look.

" What is all this ?" he asked. "Charlie ! is this the way you entertain your
guests, sir—by boxing them ? I am
very much displeased !"

" But, sir," said Charlie, sobbing, "he was so rude to poor Dora—so unkind, I could not help it."

" You must learn to curb your temper. Away with you, and do not let me see your face till to-morrow."

Charlie retired.

" As for you, my boy," continued Captain Morton to Harry, "come here and tell me what induced you to be rude to a little girl—and especially, such a good little girl as this ?" and he laid his hand on Dora's head ; but when he felt how her bitter sobs shook her whole frame, he looked up a little surprised, and asked Miss Johnson in German, what it was all about. She shook her head. "Will no one tell me ?" he said—" come Dora, you will !"

"Oh, no, no!" sobbed Dora, "I cannot help being ugly; but it was unkind of Harry to remind me of it."

"Oh," said Captain Morton, turning Harry round, "I see;" then taking off his hat, he made him a low bow—"very witty; exceedingly amusing—but not exactly gentlemanlike."

Harry turned red—so red—that he felt his very back hot. Miss Johnson, however, said something to Captain Morton, in German: on which, he smiled—" Well, enough said! come with me, Dora and Catherine, we will go and feed the swans."

So he walked away, and Miss Johnson followed slowly with Frank Morton and Harry. She began to speak with him about India, but he was so ashamed and angry, he could scarce say a word. At last, to his great relief, old John came to fetch them home; and Mrs. Morton ordered the pony-chaise again to be got ready, and saw that the children were well wrapped up against the night air; then she kissed them all, and when she came to Harry, she whispered—"Do not vex dear little Dora, as you did this evening, any more. I am sure you did not think how unkind it was, or you would not have done so."

Harry made no reply; nor did he speak a word all the way back. He pondered how strange it was that everyone seemed inclined to be sorry for him when he was naughty, instead of being angry and offended—it made him feel very strange—"But," he thought, "I have really offended Dora this time—won't she tell a tale of me when we get home: and of how she fell out of the swing to-day?"

He ought to have said—"How I threw her out of the swing to-day."

Mr. Crawford was reading aloud to his daughter and Miss Chapman, when the three children came in; there were wax candles on the table, yet, the soft moonlight came through the window, and a thousand delicious perfumes of verbena and seringa, clematis and heliotrope.

"Well, my dear loves," cried Miss Crawford, "have you had a happy evening? Did you sail the ship? Come here, Harry, and tell me how you liked Morton Castle."

Mr. Crawford took Dora on his knee, while Fred held Miss Chapman's hand. Fortunately Fred was so full of the ship that everyone listened to his account; "so then," he concluded, "after tea we went out in the garden, and—and—" He stopped abruptly, and Dora blushed, and Harry thought "Now!"

But no; Dora said gently, and truly, "We were not so happy for a few minutes, and then Captain Morton came, and showed us the swans, so we were happy again."

"Shall I ask what made you less happy?" asked grandpapa.

"Please no," said Dora, and grandpapa said nothing more.

The bell was rung for prayers, and Harry felt more strangely than ever.

Why was it that Dora never betrayed him? Perhaps she intended to tell behind his back; very likely, but he did not care—not he! Yet he could not quite harden his heart when he heard Mr. Crawford's deep but kindly voice asking God's blessing on them all, and praying that the love of God might be shed abroad in their hearts. Nevertheless he said goodnight sullenly, and went to bed.

"What a sad state that boy is in," said Mr. Crawford, as the children went away. "I wish I knew how to deal with him."

"I think Dora's method is the best," said Miss Chapman.

"And that is?" asked grandpapa.

"To win him by love," she replied.

CHAPTER IV.

THE next day was Saturday, and Harry had not many lessons to do; he showed less temper, but was troublesome enough. He liked going down on the beach, and enjoyed the fresh cool air.

When they were tired of playing, Miss Chapman read them the story of "Prince Life," a very pretty story of a prince who learns that there is nothing so wearisome as idleness, or so pleasant as wholesome work.

"I like that story," said Fred.

"It is all nonsense," said Harry.

"Why so," asked Miss Chapman.

"Because a prince never would work; he would be very silly if he did."

"Are you happiest when you are doing nothing?"

"No, I like to play best."

"Well, that is doing something, and the nearer that something is to real work, the better pleased you are.   Mr. Crawford gave you a garden next Fred's, that seaweed that lies there is an excellent manure for it, suppose you take a wheelbarrow—Dora will lend you hers—and collect some of it for your garden."

"Yes, I should like it very much."

"Then you see when you work willingly it ceases to be work, and is pleasure. God, you know, commanded man to work, and when we love God and serve him willingly, that command becomes a source of happiness to us; but when we are selfish, and love neither God nor our fellow creatures, work is wearisome, and we are miserable—at war with God and ourselves. Do you understand?"

"Yes, ma'am," said Harry sullenly, not liking the conversation; "may I have the wheelbarrow?"

"Ask Dora," said Miss Chapman.

How could Harry ask one he had so much offended?

"Yes, Harry dear," said Dora, raising her head from Miss Chapman's shoulder, for she was not very well, "you are quite welcome;" so away he and Fred ran, and very busy and happy they were for the rest of the day.

Sunday was very happy always at Fairley Cottage. The church was not far off, and the walk there by the sea-shore with the cool gentle waves creeping in with their soft murmur, and the song of the birds from the wooded grounds behind, was delightful. Then came an early dinner, and reading in a huge Bible full of pictures, which lay on a carved table in the cool shady drawing-room. Afterwards Miss Chapman sang them sweet hymns, wherein Dora, and even little Fred sometimes joined; and Mr. Crawford talked to them of a thousand things out of Bible history. Finally, after tea, they all went to church; and, oh! the sweetness

of the walk home through the fields, so
deliciously fragrant with the heavy
dew that sparkled in the rising moon-
beams like tiny diamond stars, on every
flower and blade of grass; while the
only sound, as they lost the sweet tones
of the organ, was the note of the rail,
always a late bird.

Harry was very good all Sunday—
indeed, he could scarce be otherwise at
Fairley. He was much interested in
some Bible stories which Aunt Mary
read to them: and asked Dora some
questions about the Saviour and the
children, which she was very glad to
answer.

Monday morning was rainy, and
consequently cooler; and Dora and
Fred appeared to acquire new zest for

their studies; but Harry's sad habits of inattention, gave him terrible trouble. He would not try to fix his mind on the page before him.

A dozen times did Miss Chapman kindly and gravely warn him, that she should be obliged to punish him if he persisted, and explained how easy the lesson would be if he would try and think of it only. In vain: he fidgetted and cried, and then he set to work to kick the table; so Miss Chapman ordered him to go up stairs to an empty room, that was at the top of the house, and stay there till his lesson was learnt. Harry burst into a dreadful rage, and said he would not go—"Then you must be carried," replied Miss Chapman quietly; "I am sorry to be obliged to treat you so, but it is your own doing."

When the servant came, Miss Chapman ordered old John, the gardener, to be sent for, to carry Master Vigors upstairs—and upstairs Harry was borne shrieking and roaring—though he heard Miss Chapman desiring John to be sure not to hurt him, just as kindly as if he had been good. When locked in this dull, gloomy room, Harry cried a good deal, and had a good mind to ask for his book, and then tear it to pieces; but, by degrees, he got hoarse, and tired of screaming, and began to feel very hungry. At times, he heard the voices of Miss Chapman and Fred in the garden; and still no one came near him. At last, the shadows on the wall crept half-way round on the other side, and he was quite worn out, and very, very hungry; just then, he heard a soft voice say—"Harry." He listened; it repeated "Harry," seemingly through the key-hole. "Yes," said Harry, disconsolately; "who is there?"

"Dora," was the reply. "Oh do, do be good, dear Harry. Are you not very hungry?"

"Yes, that I am. Will you get me something to eat?"

"I will ask Miss Chapman; may I say you will learn your lesson."

"I will—go quick."

Miss Chapman came herself, and told Harry that as soon as he could say his lesson he should have some dinner, and she hoped he now felt sorry for having given her the grief of punishing him.

Harry went with her to the school-room, and in ten minutes learned his task perfectly.

"You see I was right—you could learn it; do not punish yourself again. What do you think of your own conduct?"

"I was very foolish—I am very sorry," stammered Harry, more grieved to have lost the whole day in a dark, disagreeable room, I am afraid, than for having given Miss Chapman pain.

She, however, did not think so, but kissed him affectionately, and then ordered a very good dinner to be set before him.

Dora and Fred were quite happy to

see him good again, and as the evening was wet, grandpapa and Aunt Mary played bagatelle with them till tea-time.

As they were going to bed, Mr. Crawford told them, that Mr. Hughes, the clergyman who had read prayers on Sunday, was to spend the evening with them, the following Friday; and whichever of them was not good and obedient, during the intervening days, should not come in to tea.

The next day, and the next, Harry was not naughty; he found he could learn his lessons—and there was no use in trying not to do so. He was beginning to feel ashamed of being so backward, compared with the others, and to suspect it was as pleasant to please his friends as himself: moreover, on those two nights that he had gone to bed, after a good day he found it delightful not to be obliged to think of others with scorn or ill nature in order to think well of himself; so he slept very sweetly.

On Thursday afternoon the little Mortons came over to spend the day, and all went to a beautiful well, where the ruins of an old church afforded a pleasant place to dine. It was about four miles from Fairley, and Miss Crawford proposed that the children should ride there on donkeys.

To this they joyfully agreed, the gardener was sent to hire some, and their own donkey was saddled.

All those hired on the neighbouring common had side saddles, and Mr. Crawford had decided that Charlie

Morton, as one of the visitors, should have his donkey, which had a man's saddle. At this Harry was very cross and sulky, said he would rather stay at home, till Charlie very good-humouredly gave him his donkey, and then the party started.

At first they went along slowly, and though Harry would have liked to have some one holding his hand he would not admit it.

At last Charlie Morton said, "I daresay, Harry, though your donkey looks so nice and sleek he could not go as fast as mine; let us all have a race."

"Oh yes," said Fred, and off they all started, but before they had gone many yards Harry began to cry, and losing his balance in his fright, fell off over the

THE DONKEY RACE.

donkey's tail in so droll a manner that Frank Morton, who was a little behind, burst into a shout of laughter as poor Harry rolled on the soft grass.

He was not much hurt, for he jumped up and flew at Frank in such a dreadful rage that he even tried to bite his leg.

Miss Chapman and Miss Johnson came up, however, and made him leave Frank. "You must not show such temper here," said Miss Chapman gravely, "try to get the better of it. It is provoking to be laughed at; but it is wiser to join the laugh—they did not mean to vex you. You made such a fuss about having a man's saddle, that we all thought you could ride— remember, if you show such naughty temper, I must tell Mr. Crawford, and

you cannot come to tea with Mr.
Hughes, so walk quietly before me for
a little way, and think how foolish you
have been."

Harry remained silent—he was very
much ashamed of having been so
eager for a man's saddle, and then not
being able to keep on; but no one
seemed to mind him, so he recollected
it would be far worse not to be admitted to tea with Mr. Hughes, besides he
had already found he could conquer
himself, so he said, "Miss Chapman, I
will not be cross any more—let me
have Charlie's donkey, it is quieter."

"Ask him," replied Miss Chapman.
"He has given up to you once already,
and you can scarcely hope he will
again—would you do so much for him?"

Harry could not reply, nor had he the grace to ask Miss Chapman's or Frank's pardon. He was not ashamed, however, to ask Charlie to change donkeys with him.

"Yes," said Charlie, after a moment's thought, "I do not mind."

Harry felt more comfortable when he had the pommel to hold by, if the donkey trotted: so they went on thro' a beautiful wood, with a mossy bank, at one side, a bright river chafing and sparkling over and against great black stones, all wet with the spray, and shining where the sunlight fell on them through the thick branches over head; and the birds sung, and the trees gave out a pleasant perfume of the turpentine that circulates in the young larch and fir trees.   After passing this wood, they came on a large, open field, or lawn, beautifully green, at one side of which, the high, wooded bank swept round in a circle; and at the other, the river flowed.

In the middle were two or three large trees: and under them, the ruins of a small church, partly covered with ivy; at the other end of the church, was a well, surrounded with beautifully carved stone-work; and altho' it was very deep, you could see quite to the bottom, where the water welled up in waves from the source through the sand, so strong was the spring.

Then began a very busy scene—the servant who accompanied them, unpacked a basket of provisions, and Miss Johnson said—

"How nice some potatoes would be with our cold chicken: let us go explore the wood—I think I see some blue smoke curling up through the trees—and try what we can find. Who would like to come?"

Frank and Harry said they would, and Fred also: so they set off up a path, just like travellers, seeking what they might discover.

The sweet, fresh air, the bright sun, the kindness of every one about him, made Harry feel a new creature; he absolutely wished Dora had come too, instead of thinking only of himself. As they proceeded, he laughed and talked; and suddenly, Fred said—

" Miss Johnson is like Robinson Crusoe."

Now, Frank and Harry only thought of a picture in their book, of a great tall man, dressed in skins, with a hairy umbrella, and a gun on his shoulder: so they laughed very heartily, and so did Fred just as gaily.

"I suppose you are her man Friday," said Harry.

" I mean," explained Fred, " she is exploring the woods as Robinson did his island."

" Thank you," said Miss Johnson, " I know Robinson is a great favourite of yours, so I consider it a compliment."

Thus talking they climbed a steep path, and at last beheld the cottage, from the chimney of which the smoke rose. It was situated to the right of the path, up a few rough steps, and was covered with ivy and honeysuckles; but there was no sign of any one. Miss Johnson therefore mounted the steps, the door was wide open, and they could see an old woman spinning. Miss Johnson tapped at the door with her parasol, but the old woman took no notice; at last she raised her eyes, and immediately got up and tried to curtsey to them.

"I beg your pardon for intruding," said Miss Johnson civilly; "but could you allow us to purchase some potatoes."

"Glad to see you, Madam," returned the old woman, "but I do not hear a word you say."

Miss Johnson repeated her question very loud; but at the sound of strange voices a nice clean young woman came in at the far end of the cottage, and quickly agreed to let them have the potatoes and an iron pot to boil them in. She called her son, a stout lad, to carry down the pot and a kettle of boiling water, and Harry, Frank, and Fred, carried the potatoes between them.

It seemed much shorter going back; and then they had great fun seeking for sticks to make a fire under one of the outside walls of the church—they fancied themselves gipsies and wayworn travellers. Then, when the potatoes were ready, every one agreed they were the most delicious they had ever eaten.

After assisting to gather the things together, and plucking large nosegays of wild flowers, they all collected round Miss Chapman, who told them of what she had read in old chronicles of the very church on whose ruins they now looked. How more than five hundred years ago it had been part of a large monastery, and before the happy time when God had put his light into the heart of Luther, and showed him that the Bible was the only true guide for Christians, how the monks dedicated the well to the Virgin Mary, and pretended or fancied that diseases were cured by its waters, and how poor people used to come many a weary league to bathe there, and rich people were wont to give much money to them.

"But did the water really cure any-one?" asked Charlie, looking down into it.

"I do not think it cured any one really ill," replied Miss Johnson.

"Then the monks told stories," said Frank.

"Perhaps they believed the well had healing powers—for those were ignorant times," observed Miss Johnson.

"Were they not very idle and good for nothing?" asked Charlie Morton, who was the oldest.

"No," said Miss Chapman, "not always: there were many good, kind, and industrious men among them, who took care of the sick, and attended to the poor, and wrote out long histories, before printing was invented. There

is good in everything, Charlie—nevertheless, we do not want the monks
back again."

"No, certainly not," said Mr. Crawford, who had come up unperceived
with Aunt Mary.

They were joyfully received; and
then grandpapa asked what pool or
well was it that the Jews believed could
make a man whole, of whatsoever dis-
ease he had? Fred was the first to
answer—Bethesda.

Then they began to recall all the
instances of wells mentioned in the
New Testament: and it was delightful
to hear how those young memories
were stored out of that Holy Book.
Then Harry remarked how strongly
the water bubbled up; and Aunt Mary

asked the children of what it reminded them?

There was a moment's silence, and then Dora said softly and timidly: "The Living Water springing up unto Everlasting Life."

"Yes, dear child," said her grandfather, "and that Water of Life is the Exhaustless Spring of Eternal Love, that God bestows on us, demanding only that as we have freely received, so we should freely give to Him—to our fellow creatures—not thinking of self, but of our neighbours. This delicious spring does not stop to reflect:—'I bestow freshness and life on the flowers and trees around me; I cool the lip of the wayfarer, and supply the cup of the cottager, while I gain nothing from them in return, not even thanks. Why should I perpetually pour out a tide of blessings which does not seem returned?' No, for years and years it has welled up ever the same, joyous and happy in giving. So when you are inclined to be churlish and unfriendly, dear ones, think of the Holy Well, as it used to be called."

The children listened respectfully, while Harry could not help thinking how much Dora's kindness resembled the waters of the well.

Aunt Mary told them some charming stories of the monks who lived there in olden times, and a wicked Baron who persecuted one of his tenants because he would not give up a field—for which I have no room at present; and then they boiled the kettle and made tea. When this was over, it was time to return, and they found Mrs. Morton had kindly sent a large open carriage to meet them, and so, some half and some wholly asleep, they reached home, after a very, very happy day.

CHAPTER V.

THE last day of trial before the clergyman's anticipated visit, had now arrived,
and Harry determined to improve. He
found it much less difficult to avoid
naughty tempers than at first.

At breakfast, when the post came in,
there was a thin, blue, foreign-looking
letter for Mr. Crawford, who opened
it at once. "Harry," said he, when he
had finished, "this is from your papa.
He does not, of course, know you are
with me: but he expresses the tenderest

anxiety and love for you, and hopes to have good accounts when he reaches England—as he talks of leaving India soon: feeling, I am sorry to say, very unwell."

When Harry heard this, he burst out crying—for he loved and respected his father greatly; and remembered with shame, how badly he had kept the promise he had made at parting, to be obedient and good.

Every one was most kind to him, and he was very diligent (for him) at lessons.

After dinner, Aunt Mary and Miss Chapman went into the neighbouring town; Mr. Crawford retired, as usual, to his study; Fred and Harry went to weed their gardens; while Dora re-

mained in the house to read a new book
Mrs. Morton had sent her.

As Harry was hard at work in his
garden, he espied a huge spider spinning his web from branch to branch
of a laurustinas; now, as Harry had
been used to see dreadful insects, when
quite a child, in India, he did not mind
spiders, in the least, but he remembered
that Dora had a great dread of them,
and as he knew she was in the school
room, he thought it would be good fun
to frighten her. " Is this right ?" whispered conscience. " Pooh! there can
be no harm in such a trifle," said self-
will; " there is no real danger. Dora
is only a foolish little thing." Conscience tried to say something about
the real harm of trifling inconside-

rateness, but Harry would not listen: he, therefore, caught the spider, and walked off with his prize.

Dora was reading so attentively that she did not hear him enter, and he was close by her before she looked up.

"Look, Dora," he exclaimed, "what a pretty present I have for you!"

He opened his hands just near her face. She started up, crying "Don't, Harry! Oh, please don't!" and tried to run to the door, but Harry sprang between her and it, laughing at her terror, and threatening to put the spider on her; she retreated towards the fire-place, entreating him not to come near her. "You cannot think what a horror I have of spiders; it makes me ill to see one—do go away!"

But no! the cruel boy only drew nearer slowly, with the spider stretched out just going to put it on Dora's neck, when, to his surprise and horror, she suddenly ceased to speak, turned deadly pale, and fell down quite flat in a kind of fit. At this you may be sure Harry threw away the spider fast enough; he at first thought that Dora was dead, and he was going to call for help, but he saw she moved, or rather breathed, and his next fear was for himself, he therefore threw himself beside her, calling out, "Dora, dear Dora, I have put it away, quite away. Do look up and forgive me!"

"Ah, Harry," said Dora faintly, and opening her sweet blue eyes, "how could you be so unkind! You know I am so afraid of spiders!"

x

"But I did not think," said Harry; "so Dora, do not tell, there's a dear girl—do not tell: or Mr. Crawford will never let me come in to tea to-morrow evening."

"I will not tell," said Dora; "but, Harry, never frighten me again."

Harry promised readily enough, and then went out, a good deal quieted and sobered, to his garden; while poor Dora rested her aching head on the school-room table, and had a good cry.

Harry was very sorry he had frightened her: he felt, that if he now saw any one else going to do so, he would prevent it—and he was gentler and kinder to Fred, all the rest of the day.

On Friday, after dinner, Mr. Crawford

asked how the children had conducted
themselves?

"Very well indeed," replied Miss
Chapman; "and I have an especially
good report to give of Harry, who has
behaved with more gentleness, obedience, and courtesy."

Harry trembled—how little he de-
served this praise! and how easily Dora
could destroy all Miss Chapman's good
account of him. He looked at her in
terror, but she replied by a look so
kind, so pleased, as if rejoicing to hear
him praised, that he suddenly felt as
if light had shone in a dark place—
showing him how unkind, and worthless,
and selfish he was, compared to her;
and he thought—"I will never vex
her again."

In the evening Mr. Hughes came as anticipated : he was a mild, gentle, small person, with a soft voice that sounded pleasantly. The tea was laid in the pretty drawing-room, which was decorated with flowers. Mr. Hughes was very grave, and when the children came in he was engaged in conversation with Mr. Crawford, and did not seem to see them; but he did, for when he had finished speaking he called Dora to him, and laid his hand on her head as though blessing her; then Mr. Crawford said, "Come here, Harry. This gentleman knows your father very well. Do you see any likeness in the son, Mr. Hughes?"

Mr. Hughes drew Harry to him, and parted his hair on his brow, looking steadfastly in his face, and then said slowly, "Yes; and if the heart were as good as that of his father the likeness would be stronger."

Harry looked up in his face so calm and searching, and felt himself as it were compelled to ask, "Did they tell you I was a very naughty boy, Sir?"

"No one told me anything about you, my child," said Mr. Hughes, smiling very gently. "But do you not know that the heart forms the face in its own likeness, and the best way to grow beautiful is to grow good."

Harry was much struck by this speech: and Miss Chapman very kindly hastened to assure their guest that Harry was trying to be a good boy.

Harry could but hang his head, and glance at Dora.

It would take much more time than I can spare, to tell you what a delightful evening they had—for Mr. Hughes had been a great traveller: had visited the Holy Land, and stood upon Mount Calvary. He told them all about the Holy City, of crossing the Desert, and many other things that made their young hearts beat with awe and interest.

At last, they retired to rest, happy and full of fresh thoughts, suggested by all they had heard.

The next morning, Saturday, was always one of preparation for Sunday; and while they were learning a new hymn, Miss Crawford looked in, and

said—"By-the-by, dears, if you notice
a row of small oranges on the window-
ledge of my store room, I do not wish
to have them touched—they are a
peculiar kind I have put there to ripen
in the sun."

"Very well, Aunt Mary," said Dora
and Fred.

Saturday was the day on which John
almost always drove the donkey cart
into the neighbouring market town, so
there was no one in the vegetable
garden. Miss Chapman and the two
boys went down to the shore after
dinner, but Mr. Crawford wanted Dora
to help him to put his study to rights
—a task she was very fond of.

After Miss Chapman, Fred, and
Harry had been a little while on the

shore, Harry thought he should like
to have his spade to dig a hole
in the sand, and consequently ran
up the steps and into the house for
it.

As he was returning with the spade
through the kitchen garden, he espied
Aunt Mary's row of oranges on the
window ledge. He stopped a moment.
"They look very nice," he thought;
"one will never be missed, yet—" He
hesitated, and instead of running away
from temptation, paused, and the next
moment seized one and ran away—too
late. He ate it up on his way to the
beach; it was very bitter, though cool
and juicy. In two minutes it was all
gone, while the humiliating recollection
of what he had done—the mean theft

—the dishonesty—remained to make him miserable.

Shortly after, Dora came from the study, to plant some rose cuttings that Mrs. Morton had given her. She, too, saw the oranges, and stopped to notice how small they were: and while she was looking at them, John, the gardener, who for some reason, had not gone to market that day, also came into the garden, and spoke to her; she was glad to see him, and asked for his small watering pot, which she had not been able to find.

The evening closed in—and another peaceful day was ended.

The second Sunday Harry spent at Fairley, was very much like the first, except that it was not quite so fine:

nevertheless, Harry felt miserable and ashamed of himself—all the kindness and attention shown him, were converted by conscience, into bitter reproaches.   Not that he felt the fact of taking the orange was in itself so very bad, had he had the candour to go at once to Aunt Mary, and tell her, asking pardon for his sin and disobedience.

The children had scarcely begun their lessons on Monday morning, when Aunt Mary came into the school room rather hastily, saying—"Which of you, my dears, took an orange from the window-sill?—for there is one missing, and no one knows anything of it.   Did you, Fred?"

"No, Aunt Mary."

"Did you, Harry?"

He hesitated—he did not like to forfeit his new character, so he answered hesitatingly " No."

" Well, Dora, I know you would not," to which Dora, a little ashamed of being thus addressed, as if her Aunt had more confidence in her than the rest, made no reply.

" It is very strange," said Aunt Mary, and she went away.

Nearly half an hour elapsed, and then a message came from Mr. Crawford to request that Miss Chapman, Dora, Fred, and Harry, should go to the study.

They found grandpapa seated in his arm chair, with Aunt Mary standing beside him, and John opposite. "Come in, my dears," said he. "I want to get at the truth of this affair.   Your Aunt says she counted her oranges about five o'clock on Saturday evening —there were then two dozen and a half; a little after six, the sun having gone off that end of the house, she took them in without counting, put them into a cupboard, which she locked, and left the store-room, which no one entered till she did herself this morning, when there were but two dozen and five oranges.   Now these things are sometimes a temptation to such young creatures as you are, therefore do not fear to speak the truth.   I wish to clear up the affair.   I know you boys were on the beach at that time."

"Yes," said Miss Chapman, " they were with me."

No one seemed to remember that Harry had come up for the spade.

"Now, John, what have you to say?" asked Aunt Mary.

"Why ma'am," said John, speaking very reluctantly, "about half-past five I came into the garden, after fixing the gate into the paddock—and a troublesome job it was—I see Miss Dora walk right up to the window and stop before it. When she heard my step, she turned round, startled like, and asked me for the small watering-pot. I gave it to her, and went to weed the spinach, while she was a planting the roses."

"My dear child," said Mr. Crawford gently but gravely, "it looks very much as if you took the orange. Did you?"

L

Dora was a nervous child, and she felt so agitated—so fearful that her beloved grandpapa should think her guilty—that her " No, grandpapa," came out so tremblingly Mr. Crawford did not know what to think.

" I am infinitely distressed, Dora," said he, " I fear I cannot believe you."

At this, Dora hid her face in her hands, and began to sob bitterly.

Meantime, Harry's heart began to throb, and all Dora's kindness and forbearance towards him, came into his mind. Should he speak out ? "What! and lose your good character?" said self-love. " But," suggested sincerity, " is such a character worth having?" " Dora would not act thus," said conscience; "did she not always love you?"

"I fear," continued Mr. Crawford, "I must speak to you seriously, and alone—so leave us, please."

Miss Chapman rose to go: and poor Dora sank on her knees in an agony. One moment more, and to the astonishment of every one, Harry sprang forward, exclaiming—"I did it—I did it; do not punish Dora, please, Mr. Crawford. I do not care what you do to me—I am naughty, and told a lie to Aunt Mary; do what you like to me, but do not punish Dora!—dear, kind Dora, who forgave me for throwing her out of the swing, and imitating her at the Castle, and nearly frightening her to death on Thursday, with the spider. And you will love me still, Dora?"

Dora ran to him, and clasped her arms round him: "Yes, yes! dear Harry—I always loved you, and we will all love you! Will you not forgive him, grandpapa?"

Mr. Crawford was silent for a moment; and then said—"I do not think a boy who shows such penitence, is in danger of committing a similar offence again: therefore, I do forgive you dear, child, and pray God to bless you, and make you a true and honest man."

Then Harry kissed Miss Chapman and Aunt Mary, and said he would try and return the great goodness they had shown him, by being obedient and kind; and then he cried very much

—feeling how good-for-nothing, and naughty, and undeserving of every kindness, he had been—yet, happier in this humility than he had ever been before.

Never had Harry spent so sweet an evening as that which succeeded this scene.—The sunshine seemed brighter; —the blue sea more sparkling—the song of the birds more sweet than they ever were before. He was at peace! for God had given him grace to overcome 'self.'

He now became the fast friend of Dora and Fred, and quite as ready to give up to them as they were to him.

His lessons grew to be a pleasure rather than pain, and though occasionally idle and a little cross, these faults he was daily conquering, and he was ever ready to confess himself wrong, and try to amend.

His very looks improved, and the next Sunday when Mr. Hughes overtook them on their homeward walk after church, he exclaimed, " Why you are twice as like your father as you were last week, my boy !"

A few days after this, as the children were very busy helping John to clear away the grass he had mown on the lawn, a carriage drove up, out of which stepped a tall, thin, pale, weak-looking gentleman. He went into the cottage, and, after about half-an-hour, the children were sent for.

When they entered the dining-room

Mr. Crawford said, "Harry, look here!
Who is this?"

Harry looked and hesitated, the gentleman opened his arms, and then
Harry, shouting "Papa! papa!" sprang
into them.

It was indeed Harry's papa, who had
left India shortly after writing the letter
which had reached Mr. Crawford only
a fortnight before.

"And now," said he, after kissing
Harry fondly over and over again, "am
I to rejoice over a good boy, or mourn
over a bad one?"

"Rejoice," replied Mr. Crawford,
"over an honest, kind boy, who ear-
nestly strives to conquer himself."

"My child," said Mr. Vigors,
"these words are of more value to

me than all the kingdoms of the earth!"

Never had Harry dreamt of anything approaching the happiness of this moment—new life seemed to dance in his heart and sparkle over everything.

"I am so glad you are pleased, dear papa," said he, "but I have been very naughty, and did not care for anything but self. Grandmama was always scolding me, and at school they flogged me, but when Dora loved me so much I had no heart to be naughty any more."

"So it always is," said Mr. Crawford, as Aunt Mary and Miss Chapman finished giving Mr. Vigors a history of Harry's visit to them, after tea, as they sat in the open window, through which came the delicious perfume of the new mown hay, the flowers—and the last sweet notes of the thrush—" the heart may resist fear, and anger, and punishment, but nothing can harden itself against the melting ' POWER OF LOVE.'"

FINIS.

LaVergne, TN USA
27 September 2010
198702LV00002B/32/P